STRAIGHT OUTTA

BRENDAN MURPHY

Brendan Murphy is a freelance photographer based in Belfast. He has previously worked for the ***Daily Mirror*** and ***The Irish News*** as both photographer and Picture Editor. His career in photo journalism has spanned four decades, running parallel with some of the most tumultuous periods in the north, resulting in many awards for outstanding photography.

COLIN SLOAN

Colin Sloan collaborated with Brendan Murphy by writing the poems and prose for their first book: ***From Lambeg To The Drum, A Lyrical Journey.*** Colin worked in Belfast city centre for sixteen years and with Brendan got to know and gain the trust of many of the characters portrayed in this book.

STRAIGHT OUTTA BELFAST

COLIN SLOAN

—

BRENDAN MURPHY

THE BREHON PRESS
BELFAST

First published 2007 by The Brehon Press Ltd
1A Bryson Street, Belfast BT5 4ES, Northern Ireland

ISBN: 978 1 905474 219

Printed and bound by Nicholson & Bass, Belfast

Ulsterbus Ltd. Board SE No. 72055

1984-85

Validity Mon. - Fri.

Name Colin Sloan

School Methodist College

Home Stage Ballyskeagh

School Stage Belfast

D.O.B. 5.9.66 Route No. 24

This Pupil's Sessional ticket is not transferable, it must be presented on each journey and must not be removed from cover. For conditions see over.

If found please return to any Ulsterbus office.

CONTENTS

CONTENTS

The star of evening slowly rose,
through shades of twilight gleaming,
it shone to witness Erin's woes,
her children's life blood streaming:
'Twas then, sweet star, thy pensive ray,
fell on the cold unconscious clay,
that wraps the breast of Betsy Gray,
in softened lustre beaming.

MARY BALFOUR

ACKNOWLEDGEMENTS

This book would not have been possible without the help of the following people;

Damian Keenan, Brendan Anderson, Michael Faulkner, David Martin,
Brian Knott, Eleanor McCann, Heather Finnigan, Janet Artherton and Julie Reid.

FOREWORD

This second collection of poems and images by Colin Sloan and Brendan Murphy is not just highly readable – it is, on several levels, deeply affecting. If you have ever looked at a face in the crowd and wondered, 'What's your story?'; or grappled with notions of tolerance and empathy, of love, passion and the passing of things held dear; above all, if you see Belfast as an old friend who has been through a great deal and is emerging with bewildering haste into a bright but mildly unsettling future – then these poems will strike a chord.

The most satisfying thing, though, is the sheer quality of observation. As a rule, the rest of us take a wide-angle view of things. We look but we don't see; or rather we see only the general – crowd, the street, the city at night – at the expense of the particular. 'That woman in the crumpled summer dress' in the poem Street Musician, who 'files her way home without paying any heed to the tangible resonance that follows her down the street' is you and me. We tend to forget that every crowd is a collection of individuals, with individual stories, and we miss the little dramas that play out around us.

Not so in this collaboration. With uncanny consistency, Brendan Murphy's shutter reduces the moment to its essentials and offers us a precision-cut, wafer-thin slice of very real life; and Colin Sloan's words – spare, honest, elegant – give it voice. In the same poem the busker, who 'settles for an easy rhythm casting shadows on the street', and produces sounds 'that fold latitudes and continents into one', is clearly the star; but without the walk-on parts of the blue lady, and the café-goer in the shadows who swings her teabag-on-a-string absently between thumb and forefinger like a metronome, the piece would be little more than a great picture with a caption.

As elsewhere in the collection, the key elements are so subtly articulated by the balance of words and image that we are encouraged to linger, to look again, and with each visit to find something new – as good a measure as any, perhaps, of the poet's or the photographer's art.

MICHAEL FAULKNER

Station
Tourist

PREFACE

I could set out in any direction with Brendan and by the end of that day's walk he would have taken enough images to give life to many volumes recounting the things that we often overlook or just take for granted. He has that inquisitive eye which lifts events and details out of the ordinary, he often waits or revisits places that he knows might yield something worthwhile. I tag along, he introduces me to the characters he has got to know, we gain their confidence in conversation and I try to glean something of what they have experienced.

The hard bit for me is the images we have to pass on; Brendan has so many that it is a bit daunting. Most capture the essence and sense of place about Belfast. This is a very big canvas to try and write about, so many details can easily be overlooked, so we try and personalise it through individual stories and accounts. We tried to portray a city in transition, emergent, through the eyes of different generations and how they sought to deal with irreversible change.

So what we have tried to compile in this work is a snapshot of daily life for a set of very different individuals and related places that we might be very familiar with already, but that have been embellished through these atmospheric photographs and given me a tale to tell. Many of these characters and places are vulnerable, we can only try and document them here so that they are not overlooked and forgotten.

In this city's haste to throw off the shackles of the past, it runs the risk of losing much of the personality that created its own unique blend of self deprecation and stoicism. Belfast is experiencing rapid growth and economic investment that was unthinkable until recently; this boom in development is changing the landscape and communities.

The Troubles may be behind us, but they shaped the thoughts and memories of different generations and the new progress which is to be welcomed has also swept away a lot of the landmarks of the past which to many were held in regard as reassurance to the uncertainty of change.

COLIN SLOAN

THE OUTDOORS STORE
millets
ENVY
outdoors

For

Sheelagh

DRIVE TIME

They picked out the cobbles, outlines and tracks
where the trams could once gather speed
lending romance to the post-war gloom
of sodden Mac's, brollies and Trilby hats.

They widened the path to meet the need
to soothe the flow and fall of feet,
that shell of a showroom with open air accommodation
gives up its gable walls in favour of a busy junction.

The traffic humps and chevrons
edged by a malady of signposts,
calming measures form a standstill,
the whirr and dirge from the car fans kick in.

EULOGY

The funeral is tomorrow
so you can collect yourself today,
think of her this evening
and what you are going to say.

The cheeky sparkle in her eyes
as she joined the queue without buying
just to see me on a work day
to make me smile without even trying.

What a catch she would have been
in Bank Buildings so long ago
or posing at the counter of the Milk Bar
while flirting with the G.I. Joes.

Death is welcome to the remnants,
let the fire consume the bones,
wrap me up in a cloth of contentment
once worn by a lady I used to know.

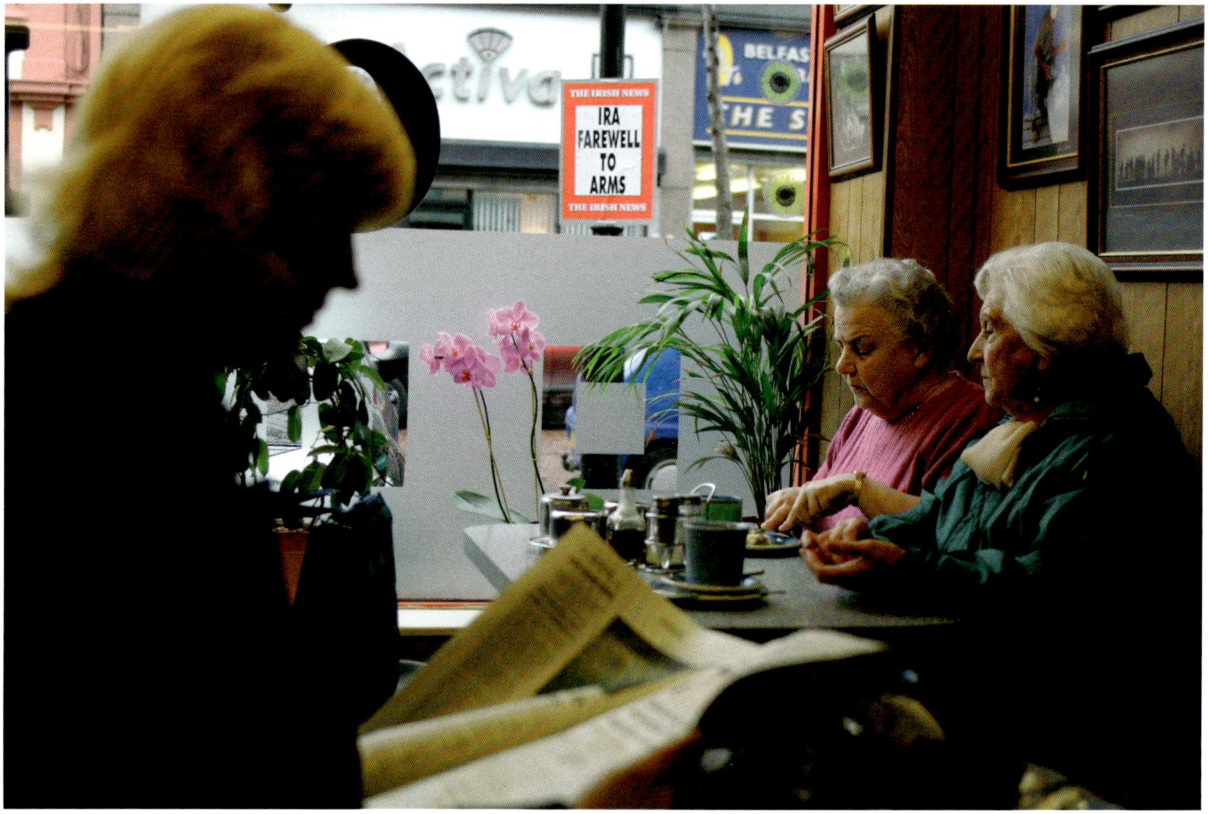
THE IRISH NEWS
IRA
FAREWELL
TO
ARMS
THE IRISH NEWS
BELFAST

FAREWELL TO ARMS

It's time to fortify that careworn expression
with a Six Counties fry and a cup of tea.
I know just the place in Donegall Street.

The papers have it right, peace is general all over the north;
we have given a high price for it, you don't have to look far:
every street that leads from here was paved and paid for by the stricken.

Where did the time go, what were we thinking?
You were the backdrop that stole my looks and youthfulness
the soundtrack for my smoke breaks, always a dead certainty.

Peace stares back at me like an unwanted Christmas jumper.
I don't quite know what to do with it, does it suit me?
One size they say fits all, let's hope they have plenty in stock.

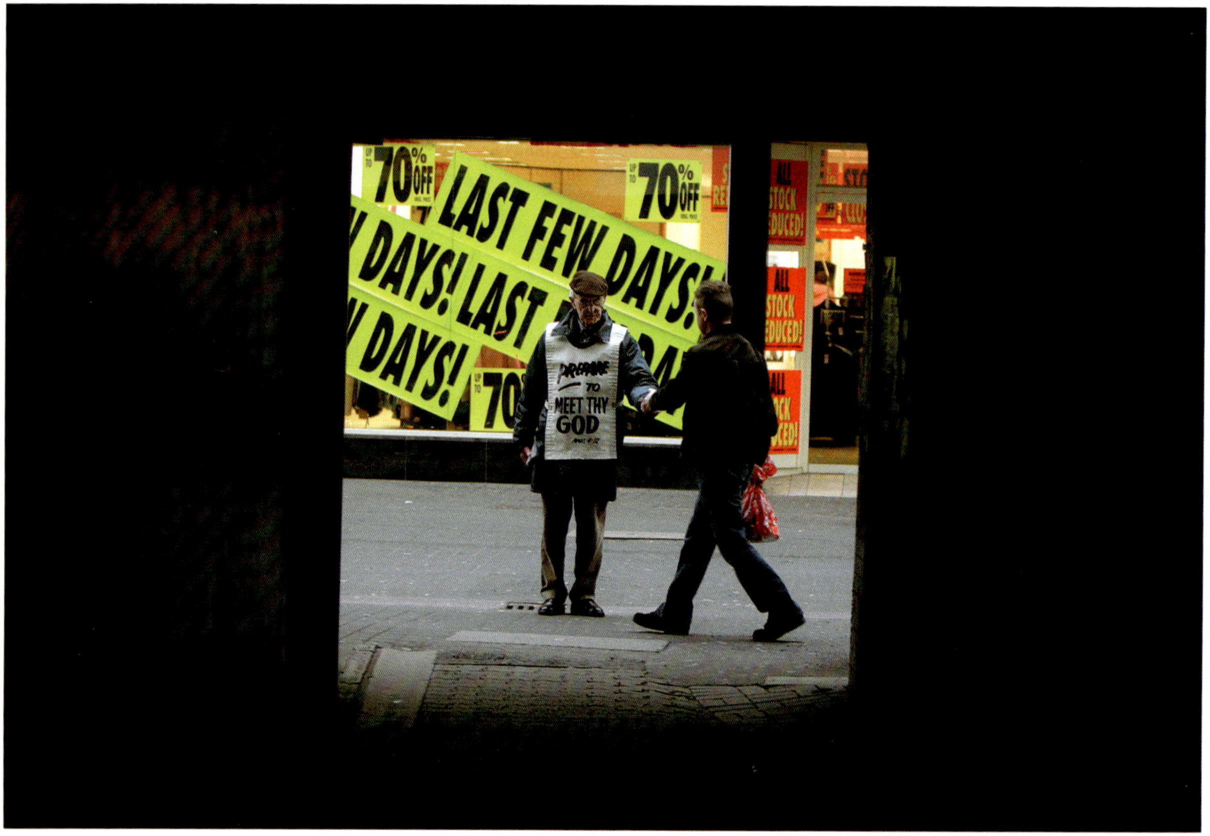
70% OFF
LAST FEW DAYS!
DAYS! LAST
DAYS!
70% OFF
PREPARE TO
MEET THY
GOD
ALL STOCK

CASTLE JUNCTION

It's lunchtime in Castle Junction
and I want to freeze this moment:
the open-top bus is in luck today,
plenty of takers for Murder Mile Revisited.

George picks his spot on the kerb across from Primark.
With a grave intent he bows to each passerby;
revolving with the flow, he hands out his sacrament,
his impermeable expression is in marked contrast
to the jacket over the shoulder office junior he has caught
blue-toothed with a cigarette, waiting for the lights to change.

On the wire bench which circles the tree near the kiosk
the man with the painted eyebrows and the toupé
which marks him out from the winos
who are steeped in Cuprinol, ready for all weathers;
the man with the painted eyebrows and the toupé
looks right through me; he thinks he could have been a contender
as he waits in the shade for better days that have been and gone.

ECCE PANUS ANGELORUM
BEHOLD THE CLOTH OF ANGELS

All too conscious
I make the sign of the cross
in this house of many mansions
drawing a palm down my forehead, across my chest
in a synchromesh of peace.

Father, when we spoke
we talked about choice and persuasion,
that I must be here for a reason
if not for me then for someone,
something pure, and lasting.

The call to Mass competes with the drone –
the reversing bin lorry beyond the door;
Chapel Lane is a bottle neck of rolling barrels,
automated shutters, delivery vans and trinket stalls.

I mumble my way behind the loud and the faithful,
offer up prayers to long lost Elizabethan Martyrs,
give thanks for Mission work overseas,
glad hand those who are immediate to me
before skipping silently out as the queue for the ash
snakes past my aisle blocking off the pew.

ILL ABOUT THE HEART

What is it about you now
that I miss, that I didn't know before?
What did you put in my drink
to make me want you
when I wasn't even thirsty?

Why do I blink first,
give in and text you
with nothing good to say?
Why do I care if you won't love me
now, later, or any other day?

Where's the future in this
when I can't remember a time
I lost my watch in the place we first met
along with all other valuables
and forgot to report the crime?

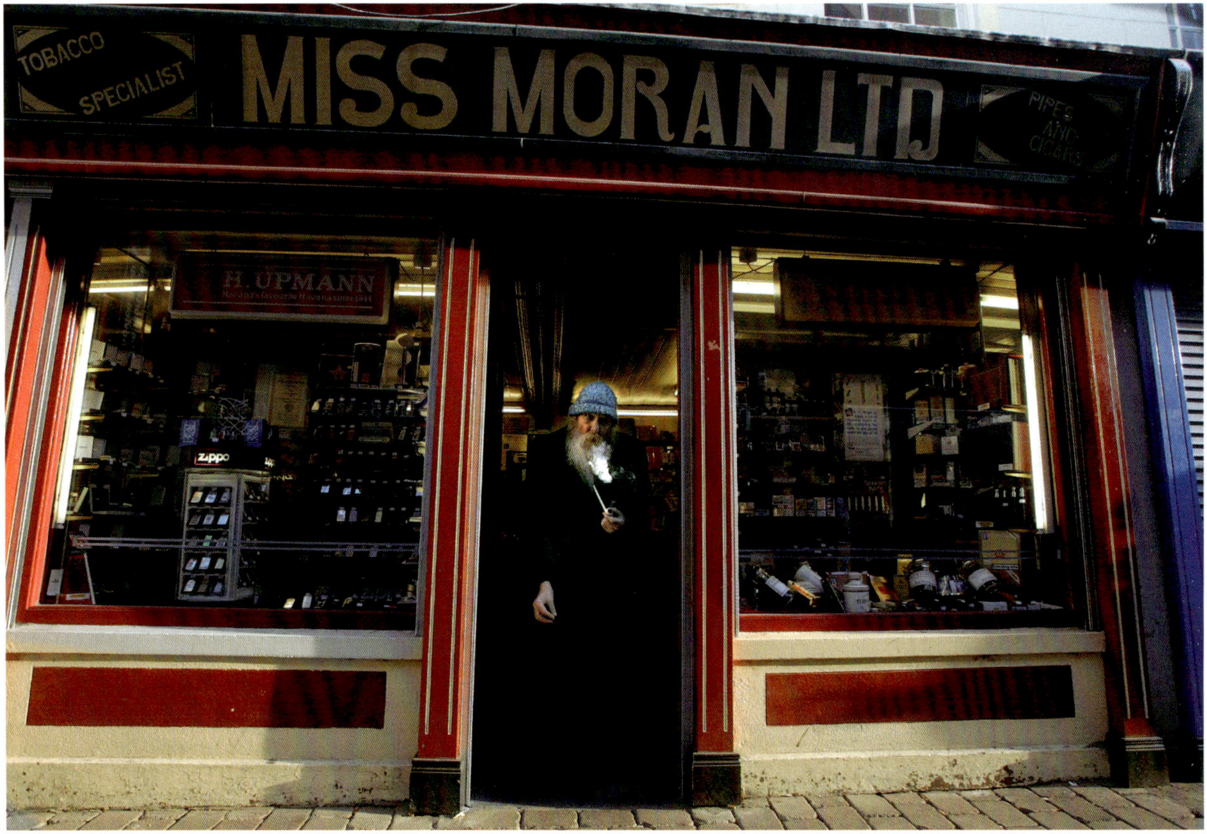
TOBACCO SPECIALIST
MISS MORAN LTD
PIPES AND CIGARS
H.UPMANN
Zippo

MR WEIR

I like the pace he takes,
measured over Cathedral steps
beyond reach of the American tourists
beneath the breathless battle flags
through the nave and empty transepts.

The regimental panes of light
lend him an accent
to speak to the god of his youth
who once gave solace amidst the chaos
under a raging sun of Aden.

Tucked away he begins,
the muttered dedication,
translucent fingers clenched
in shades of grandpa Broon.

Later, we take tea outside,
tapping the pipe in ritual acceptance as I pour;
looking at me with the trust of a child
who hides behind unbelted corduroy,
filling any gaps in conversation
with plugs of Old Virginia.

FLAT MATE

They cut off the phone today;
it's my fault I know
so you retreated to your room
with its trace elements of a Poe novel.
Pin-tacked black muslin stretches from the ceiling
over rigid sheets with the pallor of Lincoln's funeral train.

I put on the emersion and waver in the kitchen as the rot sets in,
the crunch of unswept linoleum beside the fridge
whose contents you have now labelled to remind yourself
as the bulge under the ice box gets bigger, sucking at the microchips.

The Chinese couple above cook up noodles in the early evening,
dried infusions mingle with the shadows in the yard polluted only by the Jackie Wilson record
which vibrates in time with the ceiling rose and the naked bulb in the living room.

Dirty net curtains hang limp in the draft by the open window.
I have rolled every butt in this pub-stolen ashtray, now I'm out;
feeling down the sofa, under the rug by the coffee table you fell through,
smashing the glass without a scratch, or even spilling a drop of your Tequila.

MITCHING CLASS

With a neck as brass as an Apprentice piece
I stride past the Principal's window,
gliding over ramps to the sound of egg shells,
beaking off school grounds
in mid period, to what end?

Rolling skins near the cholera pit in Friar's Bush
chilling on the lichen slabs, tearful trees in the mizzle
gaps in the tombs let in light from Landseer Street;
twisted mementos carry the death struggle to the surface,
rusting inscriptions hang loose over rotting bark.

I thaw on the wire-meshed heat pipe in the Palm House;
humid air rises through the grills in the floor,
brittle panes, toned in algae, drain from the apex.
The school project party give me a dismissive glare
marking me as a renegade and as rare as any plant in there.

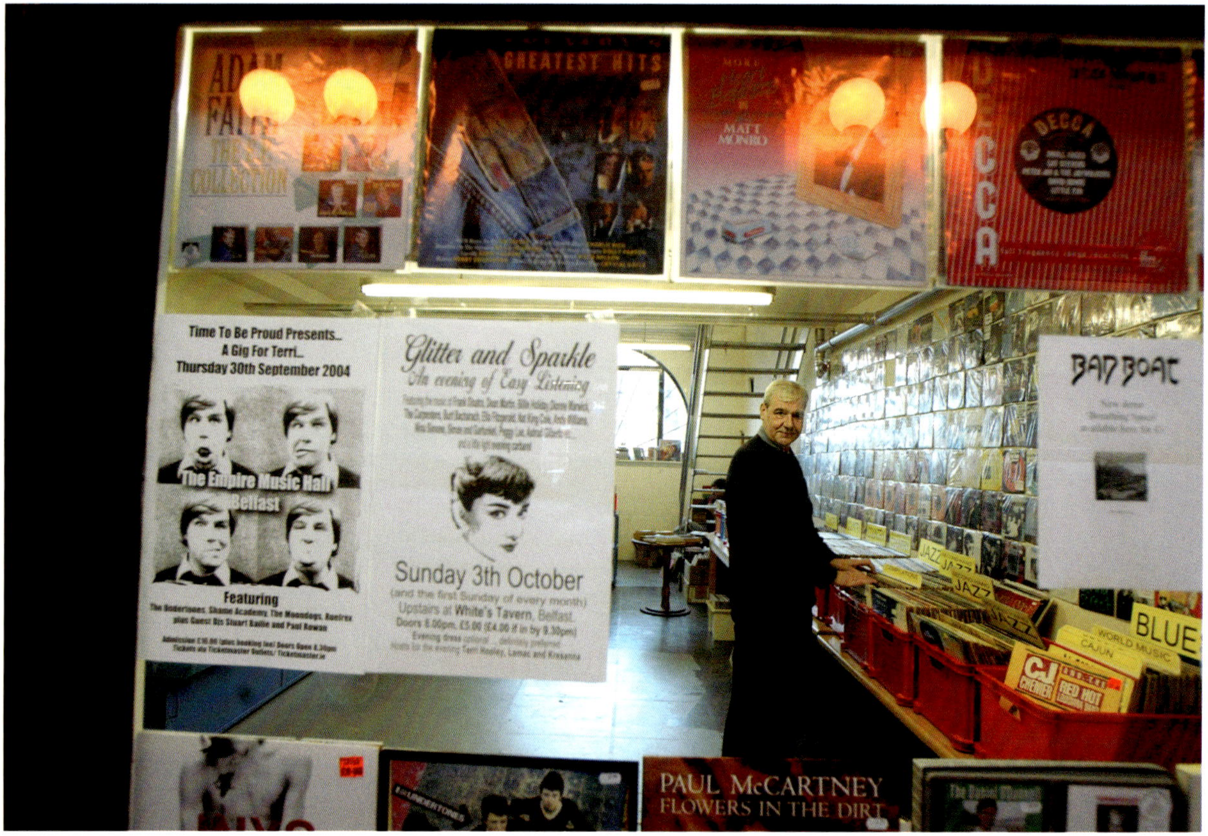

ADAM FAITH
GREATEST HITS
MATT MONRO
DECCA
Time To Be Proud Presents...
A Gig For Terri...
Thursday 30th September 2004
The Empire Music Hall
Belfast
Featuring
Glitter and Sparkle
An evening of Easy Listening
Sunday 3th October
(and the first Sunday of every month)
Upstairs at White's Tavern, Belfast
Doors 8.00pm. £5.00 (£4.00 if in by 9.30pm)
BAD BOAT
JAZZ
BLUES
WORLD MUSIC
CAJUN
PAUL McCARTNEY
FLOWERS IN THE DIRT

PLAY IT FOR ME

Elvis points the way,
creeping over threadbare carpet
up the rickety stairs past Sassafras.

Trying too hard to look like I belong,
it's as pointless as the pencils in my school blazer.
I'm out of my depth here and Terri knows it
he reels me in with his good eye...
No point in hiding behind the gatefold sleeve
of a Japanese import of Tangerine Dream.

He takes a minute to blow on the needle,
lets it fall with precision on an albino 12";
'Bella Lugosi's Dead' pounds off the walls
creating a portal to the hell mouth
half-way down Great Victoria Street.

I blurt out that I need to impress someone;
this unorthodox plea in the land of the poseurs
meets sniggers of derision during a lull in the single.
'A girl?' he smiles, compounding any injury.
'What do you think?' I parry as it limps out of my mouth,
trudging to the exit as he reaches for more vinyl.
Holding up a sleeve he shouts, 'Marvin always has done it for me.'

WHEN WE MEET

Wrap those slender fingers
around a hot mug and sit with me;
we can huddle in the condensation
keeping each other warm, smug in contemplation,
look out on a day as grey as any slate,
wiping away any doubts about our love.

Brush my leg under the table,
stroke our thighs close and long.
The room, the view and the waitress
melt in this silent ardency,
broken only by the splash on the glass
from the heaving bus lane outside.

DIVIDEND

So at a pace we didn't set
the obstacles are being dismantled,
these forts and firing positions
are seeking permission for replacement dwellings.

The grudge remains the same,
held so tight, so high for so long
but the landscape has changed,
less vigilant in shirt sleeves with a hint of toleration.

STRAIGHT OUTTA

BELFAST

PROCESSION

I only dress this way to be with you;
you kiss the mirror with my reflection
beside the garbled mess of zips and tartan.

Our heads are full of half-learnt songs
that you never play all the way through,
prising out pearls in the lyrics
as if they had been written for you.

Moving through the vapid boys and melting Goths
beneath the dead Victorians at the City Hall
teasing each in turn with a leather-laced step
they won't get a look in and their expressions show it,
but it's part of the ritual every Saturday afternoon.

NO WAY TO MEET

Hiding from your ma in a wardrobe in Harrogate Street,
loose change and latch keys spill out over the floorboards,
forgotten trainers act as bottom feeders mixing fumes with sulphur,
the Regal packet and matches riding tight across my chest.

My God she's staying! I can hear her fill the kettle, the first of many.
She'll drink tea in the yard with a fag by the kitchen door
wearing that Columbo-coloured overcoat and expression to match.

A speckled moon through the slit in the keyhole, the width of my numb finger,
bony knees frame my eye-line, cutting off any blood supply,
ankles tingle and grow cold while buttocks convert to quick lime.

Coat hangers become crop dusters in poor visibility,
shoe-boxes are sleepy farmsteads with sweaters for fields and socks roam as sheep;
ties are dirt tracks with glove embankments and fur-trimmed hedgerows,
her sounds are muffled by the riverbank as I pass out beneath the bales and sheaves.

MR LAURO

I've caught him in a good mood:
coming in here by mistake in a downpour,
he lets me dry off at the doorway,
shrugging off a sigh through a magnified gaze.

I bump into the pickle helmet on the hat stand
above the trinket cases full of worn-out brass,
faded ribbons, pocket watches, sepia lockets and metal clasps
with dented cigarette cases lying next to broken flasks.

Opposition cap badges, epaulettes and arm bands
lie stacked together without sentiment
among pewter trays and flower jugs
that have all seen better days.

Dirks, scabbards and flintlocks
litter the room above the din of each clock mechanism
while the thrall from the casket light holds your attention
until the steam streams in from fresh sunlight after the rain.

STAYING OVER

Blowing smoke rings in Finbar's shed,
cadged Peter Stuyvesants off his ma
never tasted so good.

She keeps cartons of them on the stand in the hall
beside the signed copy of *Mein Kampf*
bookmark at the page
a stuffed owl cranes with it's unsettling gaze.

A powder coated duvet, gently sieved
rises with the treeline
reaching the Emperor's old clothes
peppering his tailcoat and crooked nose.

Staring over at the house in the moonlight,
waiting for his parents to go out so we can raid the fridge,
maybe steal a couple of tins and play Moving Hearts at full volume.

MATCHWOOD MAN

The high watermark of your occupancy,
the careful deconstruction
take a beam, spare a joist,
patch up the felt, dead head a nail,
leave a rat run the width of two floor boards
over pipes of sweating verdigris.

Soot-covered webs on exposed brickwork
where the skirting boards should be,
missing pegs on a buckled stair rail,
splintered pallets and other timbers
form a queue for his fire on the living room floor.

This tenant can't even sit
hidden behind the last door to burn,
doing hop-scotch on the landing
to negotiate through the rooms,
hoarding tins on the greasy oil-cloth,
falling asleep on bales of faded newsprint.

ROUGH TRADE

It would be easier to scrape the gum off Royal Avenue
than to make a living like this;
time-served carvings
face the feckless scrutiny,
the rancour and cynicism, if only transient,
that occur in this market place.

You have to take it on the chin in all weathers,
the throw away remarks about origin,
and places that you have never even heard of
that are as far apart as the smile on your face.

They just can't see what you're not trying to sell
the essence of the spice of diversity that can be found
on any street corner from Camberwell to Mustique
but not here... heaven forbid.

SAVE ME FOR LATER

There's a heart-shaped space between your face and mine,
a reflecting pool of fragile intensity that derides any passing glances,
a heady distillation requiring no speech, just eye contact.

We should bottle this for later, as I'm sure we will need it;
an ointment to rub on the travails of attachment,
a soothing balm for the familiar physical overtures to come.

I will have this photograph of how you once looked at me
taken on the eve of everything we were to know about each other,
unbridled passions coming in on a slow tide to the land of the mundane.

STREET MUSICIAN

She settles for an easy rhythm
casting shadows across the pavement
where the cool and the young are gathered
tapping on their Mochas, mopping up to the beat
the onion bread, panini wrap, the vinaigrette and side salad.

That woman in the crumpled summer dress
who could pass unnoticed through a Kennedy motorcade
or make up the numbers at a Civil Rights march
files her way home without paying any heed
to the tangible resonance that follows her down the street.

Burnished light on granite, etching architraves and casement windows
adding mystery to the Presbyterian rotunda; it transports us
to leafy Arrondissements with secluded awnings and entanglements.
Delaney's becomes a film lot, with her at the fulcrum
producing sounds that fold latitudes and continents into one.

STRAIGHT OUTTA
BELFAST

SKYLINE

Look up and read this city's story
where they knelt to leave a signature
in each bust and scroll, a pigeon finds a home
above the workaday and ephemeral.

Beyond the chrome and tinted glass
remedial Band-Aids from a troubled past:
the controlled explosion, a kerbside blast
pouring shrapnel into tissue and plaster.

An altered eyeline, the street names remain
witness to the loss, the hurry for change
converting empty spaces to city lofts
with tight balconies and private parking.

those summer memories with family and friends...

RUSH HOUR

The rattled ignition,
the throb of the coach
exaggerated above the wheel arch,
knees press the match scraper,
a concentrate solution of passenger breath rolls down the pane
to the rubber seal at once soaking and cradling my elbow.

Wet dog and duffle-coats begin to bake and alter,
cheap perfume and stale cuisine,
sweaty bags of messages prop against fat ankles,
plastic bottles roll as the spluttering starts to grow.

We pull away from the kerbside and stop at the lights,
the briny man with a clammy bottle of Powers
offers a swig to the medical student, who declines;
those affronted at the back avert their eyes in judgement as we shunt.
Progress is slow, six miles to go and a body spreads out in every row.

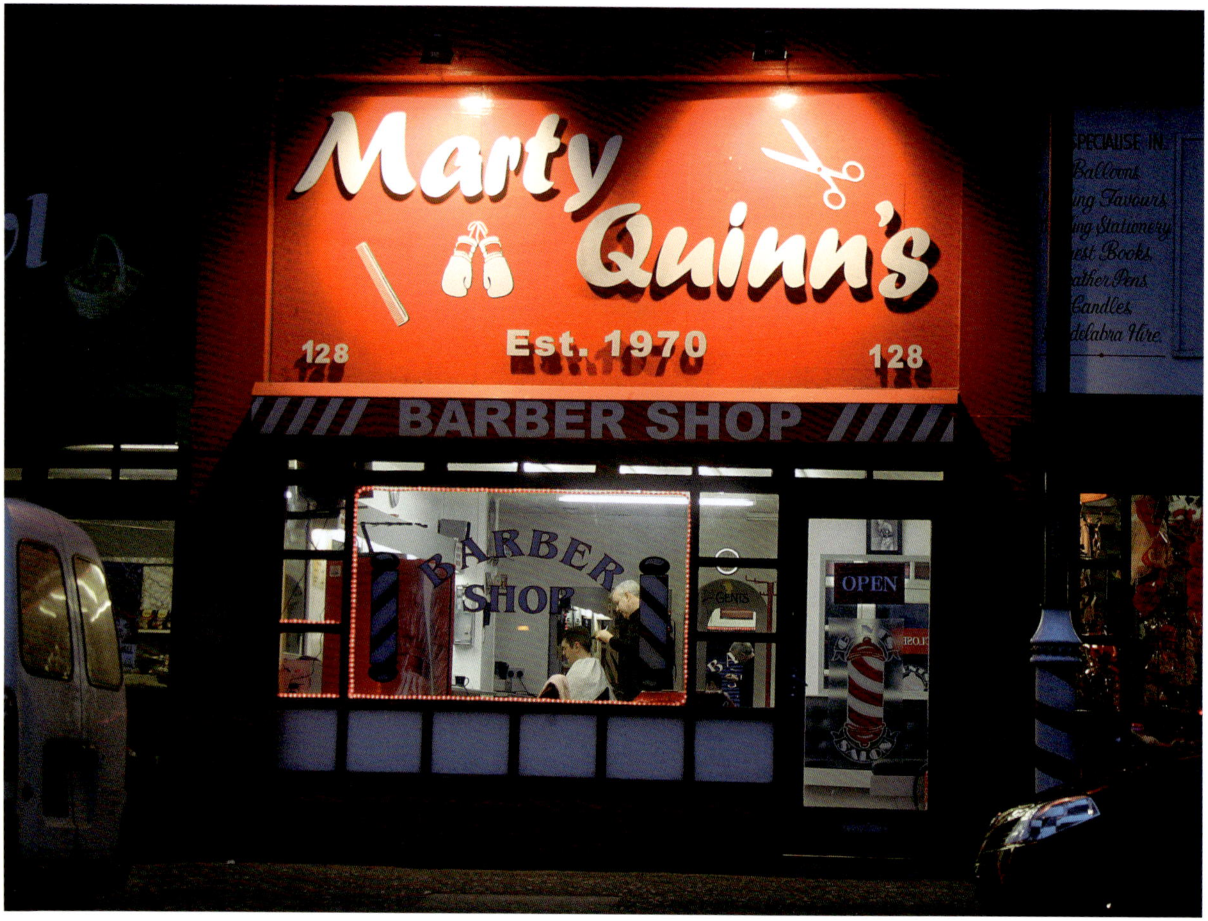
Marty Quinn's
128
Est. 1970
128
BARBER SHOP
BARBER SHOP
OPEN

PRINCE HAL

Mr Hardy produces the smoothened plank,
rests it on the red leather arms and beckons;
my exit is blocked by the thick-set man with the raincoat;
another Plantagenet haircut seems inevitable,
unless I feign injury and take my chances
beneath the seats where the loose chunks of hair meet the terrazzo.

My conversation dries up as he reaches for the shears,
my conversion to Hal Prince of Agincourt imminent,
I focus on the swirl of the red and white motif:
it crests the wall near the door to this battleground,
becoming blurred by the rain streaming down the window.

Holding court in a booth lined in sky blue formica;
my every need taken care of by Good Nell,
striking the ribs on the brown bottle of Fanta
itching loose hair from my collar,
my sceptre and orb are made of salt and vinegar.
I rake for a crown through the bones of a fish.

MR UNLIVE

His tour begins at night
in one of the many broken veins
that run off Ann Street.
With his back to the pub
he does a head count,
hushing whispers in the drizzle,
eyes close in on broken wall tiles,
errant tree ferns and dripping sea slime.

He can hear the Farset beneath the culvert
flowing freely to Prince Albert,
shows me the splinters from the clamour
above the gallows for Henry Joy,
remembers the cheers from the Reform Club
for the Mafeking defenders,
recalls the slow drum on a gun carriage for Carson.

He cups an ear in the direction of the hum
where the Heinkels dropped their payloads,
covers his mouth from the chain dust along the slipway
while the riveters watched her fateful sea trials,
conjures cordite and ethanol, pogroms and bigotry,
mixing smells in the makeshift mortuary
as the Lockout held and Larkin railed on the Custom House steps.

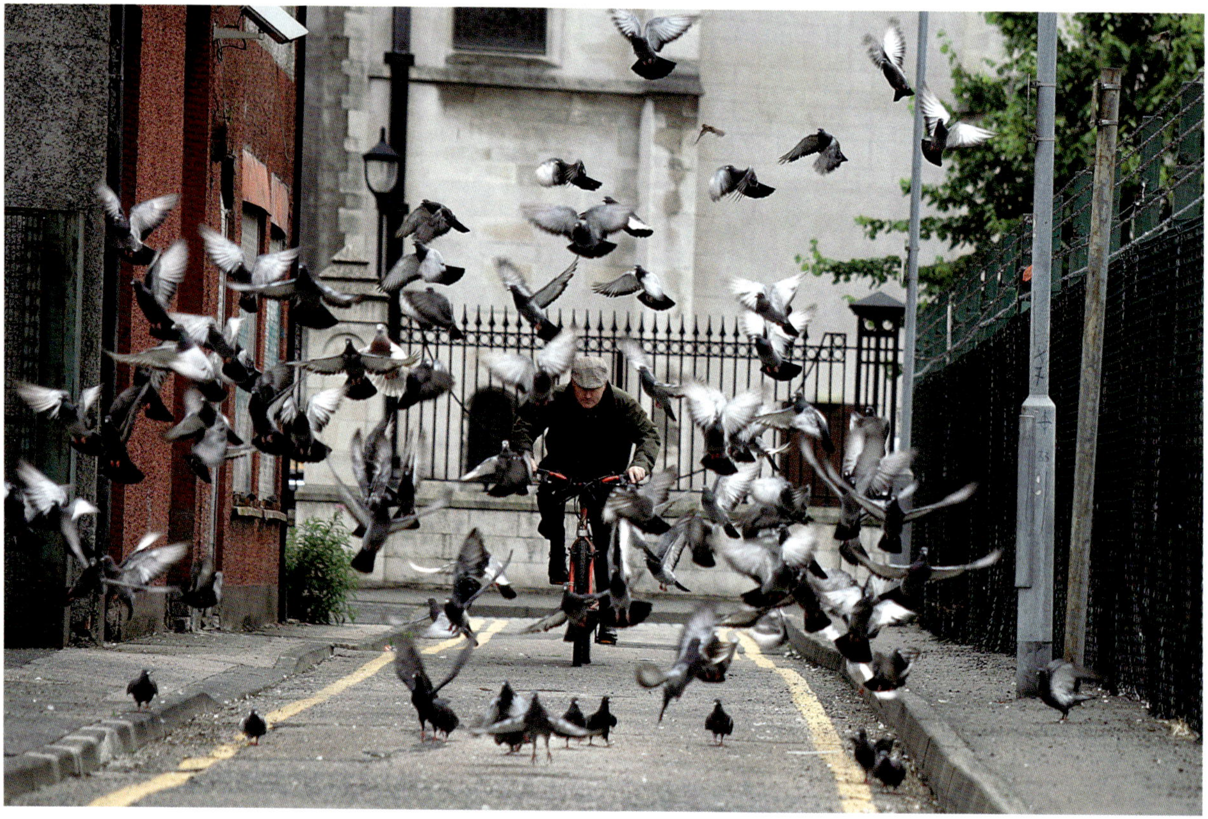

STRAIGHT OUTTA
BELFAST

LASTING IMAGE

I caught up with you in an unguarded moment
using the foot scraper at the Gate Lodge to Botanic Gardens,
tying up laces with your back to me, slightly stooped
you had been walking for too long and it showed.

My swagger soon took a nose-dive
as we made our way to the Jaffa Fountain
through the vacuous embankment hiss,
pausing as you tried to negotiate with a limp.

Your face betrayed any unspoken recollection
and my mind played tricks until I knew
this was all my fault, my selfish actions.
Me, the drunken prick, who fell through the back door
numb to the shards as I reached out for you.

You picked yourself up then and held me,
put me to bed in an attic room where you couldn't even stand;
you told me that I would always have a roof over my head
and I wore the safety of your words like a charm around my neck,
panel beaten by time but still redolent of you.

MERSEY STREET

The pleated rows
of neat terrace homes
once huddled to burn their coals
from the Oval to the cranes.

This brown field site
ringed for change
that you call a playground;
same back drop, different cast,
no quarter given to Mersey Street.

LAST NIGHT'S FUN

Your heels scraping the tables
while I climbed the pillar,
the poet on his knees in the yard
collecting false teeth by torch-light.

The actor's chosen words
consign another pint to history,
the couple nobody knows
make out on the steps, half in, half out,
blocking the doorway.

Those two in the loo
compare notes, fill in the cracks;
we dance to the end of time
in tune with the fiddler
who skids on a vol-au-vent.

ALL THE SIGNS ARE GOOD

Two Dogs is reading my palm.
Once fertile plains, now arid and wrinkled,
cupped in a wrist, a dried-up riverbed
as deep as a spoon.

I'm sure we look a sight:
he presses me intensely for details
in a huddle by the bookcase on the mezzanine,
circles in the air above my Mount Of Venus.

My lifeline trickles from its source
beneath my watch strap, coarsing all the way
as it forms a narrow channel
roughly in line with Rosemary Street
and Blinkers restaurant beyond.

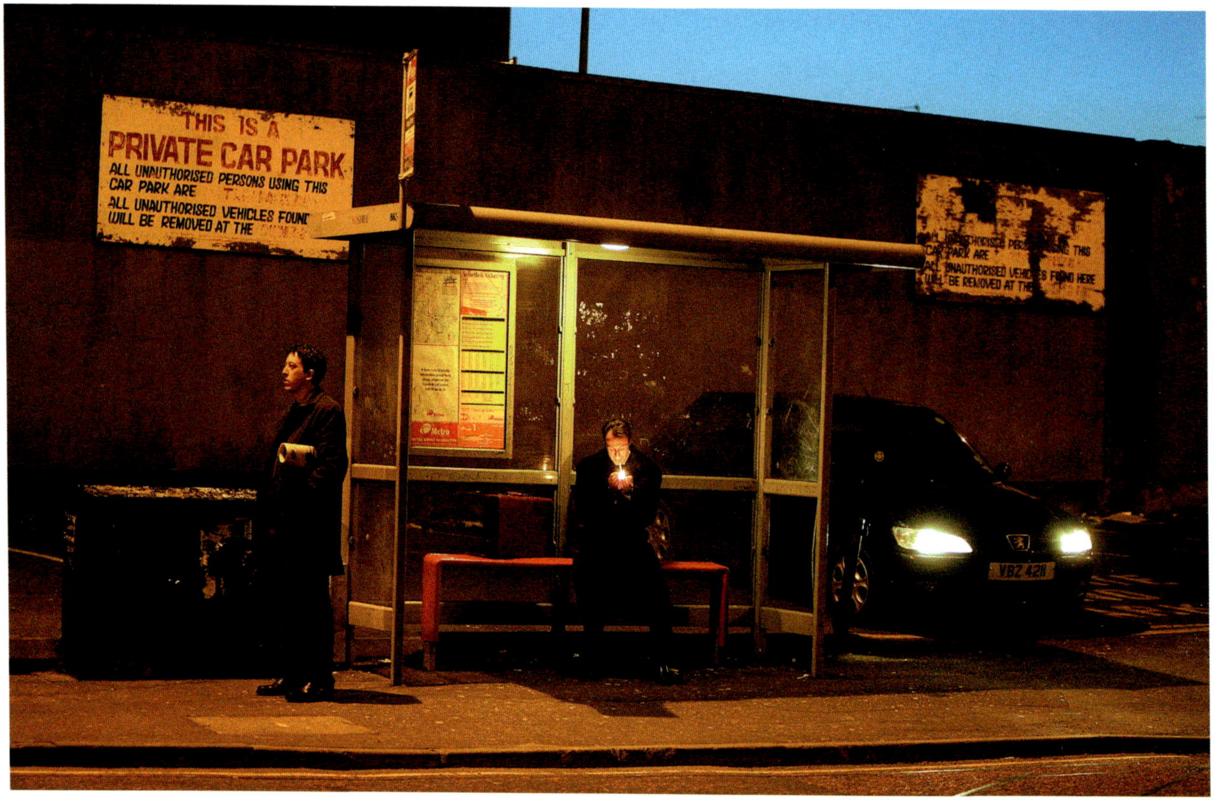
THIS IS A
PRIVATE CAR PARK
ALL UNAUTHORISED PERSONS USING THIS
CAR PARK ARE
ALL UNAUTHORISED VEHICLES FOUND
WILL BE REMOVED AT THE
VBZ 42N

DAY IN

When buses don't come in packs of three
leaving you alone to squeeze what's left of daylight
before headlights filter in and the phosphor takes hold,
watch the powder burns of jet engines over three miles high.

That tune you always hum, an album of your brother's,
Polyfilla for dead moments,
a segway from Abbey Road
has carried that weight for a long time.

There's the guy you can't stand, yer man who likes to brag;
pretend you haven't seen him for as long as you can,
nod with the iPod, fake it down the phone.
Where's the bloody bus? Too late... here he comes.

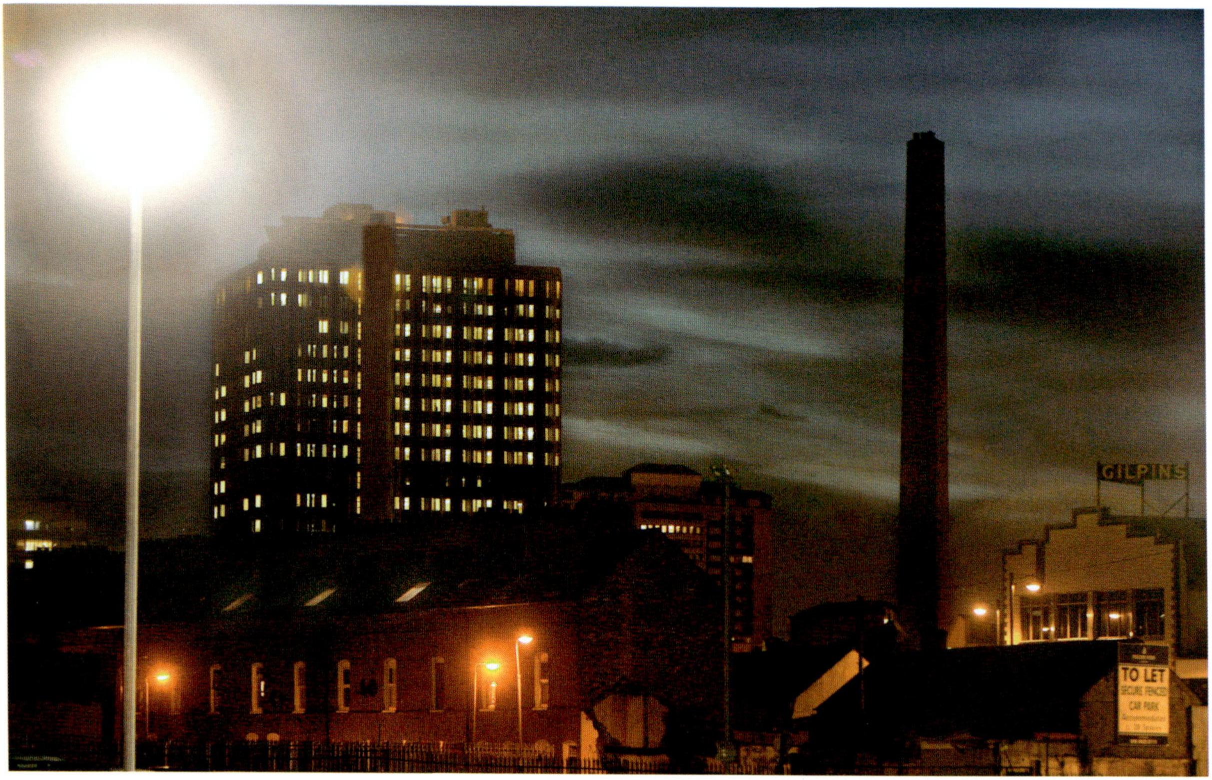
GILPINS
TO LET
SECURE FENCED
CAR PARK

WORKING DAYS

The hurried anticipation brought about from
short winter days, under clearing skies
that just about tolerate the scale of this place
as the year reaches its climax over a changing city.

Bathroom windows soon steam up from the backyard returns,
the fight for the hot water and the sink begins in earnest,
jackets and ties lie dormant on the stair rails
as the toast pops up during the subdued traffic report,
recalling delays over the Westlink and Sandyknowes roundabout.

The ward lights in the tower at the City Hospital
peel open in the gloom like an advent calendar
above the coil of the rush hour that requires your presence;
the draft at the door is harnessed by the fluorescence
playing tricks in the glass near the junk mail on the floor.